Harriet Tubman

A Little Golden Book® Biography

By JaNay Brown-Wood
Illustrated by Robert Paul Jr.

A GOLDEN BOOK • NEW YORK

Educators and librarians, for a variety of teaching tools, visit us at RHTeachersLibrarians.com
Library of Congress Control Number: 2021947503
ISBN 978-0-593-48014-4 (trade) — ISBN 978-0-593-48015-1 (ebook)
Printed in the United States of America
10 9 8 7 6 5 4

> Harriet Tubman was a hero who helped free enslaved Black people from the brutal conditions of slavery.

Harriet Tubman's birth name was Araminta "Minty" Ross. She was born in Dorchester County, Maryland, to her loving parents, Harriet "Rit" Green and Ben Ross. Minty lived with Rit and Ben and many brothers and sisters in a tiny cabin that had dirt floors, and no windows or beds.

Minty was born sometime in the early 1820s. Her parents never wrote down her birthdate because Minty and the members of her family were not allowed to learn how to read or write. They were enslaved people, owned by a person who made them work in terrible conditions for no pay.

During Minty's early life, slavery existed in the United States, especially in the Southern states. Enslavers forced Black people to do hard work and often punished them severely. Enslavers even sold Black people to other enslavers, making it impossible for family members to see each other again.

When Minty was a very young girl, she was forced to take care of babies. She also had to walk through freezing water to empty muskrat traps.

As she grew, she was given even harder jobs, like plowing fields, driving oxen, and chopping wood. The work was exhausting—but Minty persevered.

When Minty was a young woman, she met a man named John Tubman and married him. Minty soon learned that she would be separated from John and her family and sold to an enslaver farther south from where she lived. She knew what she had to do—run away to a state in the North to become a free person!

Minty ran off in the dark of night. She used skills she had learned from her father—how to move through the woods, how to wade through the river to throw off any hounds tracking her scent, and how to follow the North Star.

These skills helped her hide from slave catchers, people who hunted runaway enslaved people and returned them to enslavers for rewards.

As Minty made the ninety-mile journey north, she was led by her faith and the helpful hands of the Underground Railroad, a secret group of people who helped those seeking freedom.

This group provided food and shelter, information and guidance, and even transportation.

In 1849, after a long and dangerous journey, Minty reached Philadelphia, Pennsylvania. She was a free woman! And now she would be called Harriet, after her mother.

Harriet found a job working in a hotel. Although she enjoyed being free, she missed her family greatly and decided she had to help them become free, too.

It wouldn't be easy. In 1850, Congress passed the Fugitive Slave Act—a law that allowed slave catchers to capture former enslaved people even in the free states of the North and return them to their owners.

But that didn't stop Harriet. She was fierce and determined!

Harriet became a conductor on the Underground Railroad. She guided others in navigating many miles of trails, woods, and rivers to freedom.

She traveled back to Maryland to rescue her brothers and led them all the way to Canada, where the Fugitive Slave Act could not be enforced. Harriet rescued people over and over, bringing her parents and more of her family members and other enslaved people to the north to be free.

Word spread of what Harriet was doing, and enslavers began to put up Wanted posters offering a reward for anyone who captured her. This made Harriet's work even more dangerous. But her faith kept her going.

Not only did Harriet make many trips to rescue enslaved people, but she also gave speeches about the cruelty of slavery—despite having never learned how to read or write. Harriet's fame grew, as did the respect that people felt for her.